RETREAT

MAGAZINE PRESENTS

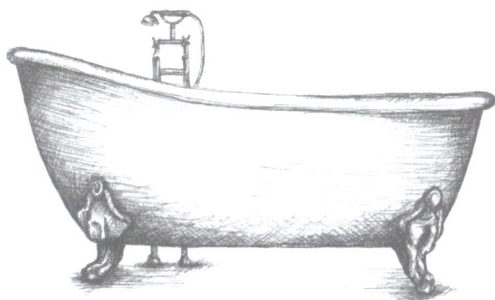

Bath Envy

THE WORLD'S MOST
EXTRAORDINARY HOTEL BATHS

CONTENTS

Vora, Santorini, Greece

FOREWORD

Hotel and Resort bathrooms are having their time in the sun. They have been brought forward in design priority from a functional requirement to an architectural highlight. Not only have our bathroom expectations become very high, as you will see they are often commanding the very best view!

Until recently, this was a different story, all but the grandest bathrooms appeared as a design afterthought. They were relegated to the back of the room, gasping for a breath of fresh air. All the tricks of extraction only resulting in an unpleasant noise and permanent dampness. Fortunately, the benefits of natural ventilation and light have been recognised and bathrooms have evolved into a staple highlight that is here to stay.

The ritual of bathing has become celebrated in the health + wellness landscape, including a high level of amenity to compliment them. Soft furnishings, delightful details, bespoke finishes, high tech appliances and conveniences, refreshments, cozy linens, privacy, connection to nature and of course, the breathtaking views.

The competition for the ultimate luxury bathing experience is hot and this new generation of hotels and resorts set the bar very high. It has been our pleasure to collate our favourite bathrooms that not only meet our new demands, but far exceed them!

Mike Dobson
Designer, StudioM1

INTRODUCTION

Hotel baths offer a wow factor all their own and have become a design statement just as integral as well-designed guest rooms. Whether it's boasting incomparable views, floor-to-ceiling windows, freestanding tubs or indoor-outdoor pavilions, hotels are recognizing the draw of an ultra-luxurious bathroom that captures the essence and history of the destination. Wash away mediocrity with these dazzling and decadent hotel bathrooms – most of which are begging to be filled with bubbles!

ASIA

Aman Kyoto

KYOTO, JAPAN

An authentic yet contemporary sanctuary situated in a once-forgotten secret garden, this ensuite is strikingly minimalist in its geometry and serves as a window onto its spectacular natural surroundings of more than 80 acres of tranquil forest.

JOALI Maldives

MURAVANDHOO ISLAND
RAA ATOLL, MALDIVES

Amid the abundant life between the palm trees, sand-covered feet and sparkling water, this over-water villa's stylish bathroom interior design encompasses marble and rose gold sinks, solid wood furnishings, outdoor and indoor showers and standalone baths with views looking out to the open ocean.

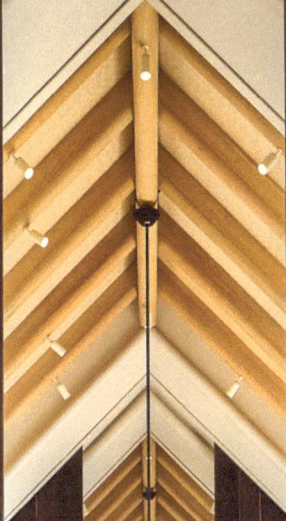

Como Uma Ubud

BALI, INDONESIA
UMA POOL VILLA

Located in the heart of Ubud, Bali, this contemporary Asian design features a fusion of traditional Balinese architecture. Featuring a traditional Balinese door and the use of a Balinese yellow bamboo woven installation as a partition between the closet dry area to the vanity and bathtub space, these elements add the cultural context of the property's location in the cultural hub of Bali.

The bathtubs were handcrafted to match the colour of the terrazzo floors in the villa and the open showers offer the charm of tropical feels, while the lush green vegetation provides full privacy in a very intimate setting. Large floor-to-ceiling windows provide abundant natural light and a combination of lush gardens and indigenous red brick Balinese walls behind the gardens elicit warm and earthy nuances.

Avani + Riverside Bangkok Hotel

BANGKOK, THAILAND

The oversized and seamless panoramic window of the River View Junior Suite allows maximum natural light flowing into the room, and provides both sunrise and sunset views with an unrivalled view of the great River of the Kings in Bangkok.

Como Point Yamu

PHUKET, THAILAND

Overlooking the Andaman Sea and the
dramatic limestones of Phang Nga Bay, this
contemporary ensuite features deep blues
and design elements drawn from Phuket's
Peranakan history.

Amankora

BHUTAN

Located in the Himalaya's sole remaining Buddhist Kingdom,
each of the five lodges, which are strategically located
across remote yet idyllic valleys, is custom-designed with
interiors by acclaimed architect, Kerry Hill. Inspired by
traditional Bhutanese forms, designs and colours, each
ensuite combines wood panelling and chocolate brown walls,
traditional Bukhari, a terrazzo-clad bath, shower, vanity and
daybed offering views across the valley.

Niyama Private Island

DHAALU, MALDIVES

Surrounded by the Indian Ocean's iconic blue topaz waters, this open-air ensuite features cutting-edge design with an al fresco rain shower.

Amanbagh

RAJASTHAN, INDIA
POOL PAVILIONS

A contemporary sanctuary surrounded by
a lush green oasis, this ensuite features
a spacious dressing area, twin walk-in
wardrobes and twin vanities. The double
doors open onto a spacious garden courtyard
boasting views of the ancient Aravalli hills.

Six Senses Ninh Van Bay

NINH VAN, VIETNAM
HILLTOP POOL VILLA

Nestled into an impressive and dramatic rock formation of the bay in the mountainous hillside overlooking the South China Sea, this unique, breezy open bathing experience offers a luxurious open bathroom with a handmade wooden bathtub and a steam shower that looks straight down on to the East Vietnam Sea.

Raffles Singapore

SINGAPORE

Following an extensive, multi-phase restoration of
the iconic, 133-year-old hotel, the ensuite features
beautiful Victorian details and Peranakan tiles as
an homage to Singapore's rich culture.

Soneva Fushi

BAA ATOLL, MALDIVES

Hidden among dense foliage within
touching distance of a pristine beaches, this
luxurious bathing experience is set within
open-air bathrooms with separate bathtubs
and showers which takes bathing to a new
dimension, truly defining barefoot luxury.

Six Senses Krabey Island

KRABEY ISLAND, CAMBODIA

Located on a 30 acre private island and blending into the lush canopy of trees, this ensuite showcases a free-standing tub with views of the natural vegetation to provide a back-to-nature tropical island experience.

Baan Banyan Luxury Villa

KAMALA BEACH, PHUKET, THAILAND
BAAN BANYAN VILLA

Baan Banyan's master suite bathrooms are masterpieces on their own; vast, decadent and supremely indulgent. Each offers a jacuzzi, twin basins and extensive use of natural stone while boasting spectacular views of the Andaman Sea.

Anantara Kihavah

BAA ATOLL, MALDIVES

Poised over the water with sweeping ocean views, a glass-bottomed bathtub ensures prime views to the marine life undersea, whilst simultaneously allowing for uninterrupted views of the Indian Ocean.

Banyan Tree Samui

KO SAMUI, THAILAND

Overlooking the azure waters of the Gulf of Thailand and nestled amid the lush jungle of a private bay in Lamai, this secluded haven offers the ultimate retreat with a comfortably-appointed double-vanity, rain shower and bath which blends harmoniously with verdant gardens and delivers the ultimate view of its tropical surroundings.

Gili Lankanfushi

NORTH MALÉ ATOLL, MALDIVES

Perched over the Indian Ocean, this rustic-luxe design combines recycled materials with sumptuous textiles in a spacious semi open-air bathroom.

KAI Sengokuhara

KANAGAWA, JAPAN

Featuring a private outdoor onsen which is filled by nearby mountain springs, this private and traditional Japanese experience boasts stunning views of Mount Kintoki and forests and offers luxury amenities and a meticulous design.

Keemala Resort

PHUKET, THAILAND

Each rustic yet sumptuous, private villa depicts the lore of
early Phuket settlers. Offering a spacious bathroom with
an indoor and outdoor rain-shower, and showcasing a
stone tub and sinks and mosaic tile shower floor, Keemla's
design reflects the Nest Clan's belief of replenishing their
soul by bathing under the moonlight.

Milaidhoo Island Maldives

MALDIVES
OCEAN RESIDENCE

Flooded with natural light and perched on the edge of the ocean, this authentically designed, thatched-roof bathroom invites nature in by opening out to the unparalleled views of the Indian Ocean, with steps straight into the water to explore the island's spectacular house reef.

Nihi Sumba

SUMBA ISLAND, INDONESIA

Blending wood and thatch construction for an open plan living that reflects the simplicity and beauty of Sumbanese architecture, this unique bathroom design features beautiful steel and stone bathtubs set amongst the backdrop of breathtaking views across the Indian Ocean.

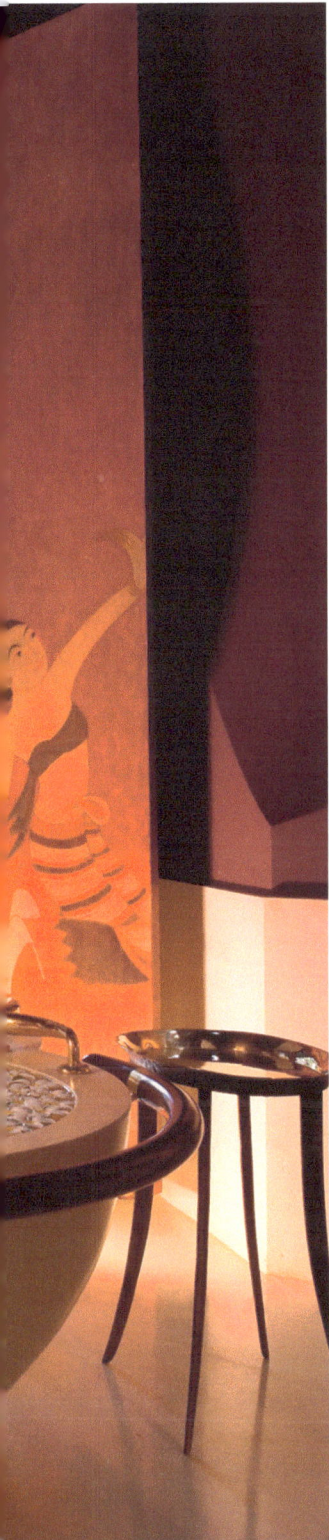

Phulay Bay, a Ritz-Carlton Reserve

KRABI, THAILAND

Nestled onto the shores of the Andaman Sea, this stunning natural sanctuary represents the intersection of nature, culture and luxury. Blurring the boundaries between indoors and out, the ensuite showcases hand-painted panels and traditional Thai design with spectacular sea views.

Rosewood Hong Kong Hotel

HONG KONG, CHINA

Situated on one of Hong Kong's most significant waterfront locations in Tsim Sha Tsui -- Kowloon's dynamic, culturally compelling heart -- the shiny marble ensuite features hammered copper sinks, beautiful freestanding white baths and dual showers.

Sheraton Maldives Full Moon Resort & Spa

NORTH MALÉ ATOLL, MALDIVES

Nestled amidst lush greenery and palm trees encircled by a crystal-clear turquoise lagoon, this Maldivian retreat features stylish contemporary bathrooms with stunning views over the Indian Ocean, complete with an alfresco rain shower and an expansive bathtub.

The Reverie Saigon

HỒ CHÍ MINH, VIETNAM
THE ROMANCE SUITE

This one-of-a-kind ensuite features rich design details which deliver an ultra-luxurious aesthetic. A extravagant porter chair sits opposite a unique inviting tub collared by Italian marble and embraced by striking red mosaic tile.

OCEANIA
&
SOUTH
PACIFIC

ESPACIO The Jewel of Waikiki

HONOLULU, HAWAII, USA

With only nine suites – each occupying an entire floor – the all-marble bathrooms are palatial with their own in-suite dry saunas, deep soaking tubs, separate glassed showers with overhead rain spouts, TOTO Washlets and luxurious BVLGARI bath amenities. With no expenses spared, even ESPACIO's plush Japanese-made towels are crème de la crème.

Kokomo Private Island Resort

KOKOMO ISLAND, FIJI

Kokomo's seaside bures (villas) are spread out across two of the island's sandy beaches. The interiors are stunningly contemporary, with bright yet earthy palettes. The oversized bathrooms feature rain showers, deep bathtubs and double vanities. Each bathroom leads out to a private courtyard with an outdoor shower.

Four Seasons Resort

BORA BORA, FRENCH POLYNESIA
OTEMANU OVERWATER BUNGALOW SUITE

Overlooking the turquoise lagoon of Bora Bora in the
shadow of Bora Bora's Mount Otemanu, the ensuite
is Polynesian at heart with décor and furnishings that
celebrate the island's natural beauty.

Little Albion

An eclectic mix of heritage and contemporary detail true to its location in Surry Hills, the ensuite's design was carefully considered down to stone junctions and solid stone hobs carved from solid marble blocks. Featuring custom brass tapware, bespoke designed vanity frames with Elba stone tops and custom-designed mirrors as a nod to the art deco era, it also displays a flawless combination of hand-painted Moroccan wall tiles and Elba solid marble floors and shower walls.

The Ritz-Carlton Residences

WAIKIKI BEACH, OAHU, HAWAII, USA

This spacious residential-style ensuite features granite and marble countertops, a separate soaking tub, and a spacious rainfall shower with views of Waikiki and the Pacific Ocean.

Lon Retreat & Spa

POINT LONSDALE, VICTORIA
AUSTRALIA

Natural stones, timbers and concretes within the building lead to the use of beautiful earthy combinations in the bathrooms such as the raw brass, matt concrete basins, matt navy and charcoal tiles, warm white stone baths, timber shelving and stumps. Boasting sunrise views over the entrance to Port Phillip Bay, the stone bath features two spouts, one which pours out mineral fed hot water directly into the tub at around 40 degrees Celsius. This mineral water, sourced from limestone caves, runs beneath the property and feeds through from the dunes.

Naumi Hotel

AUCKLAND, NEW ZEALAND

Displaying a monochromatic wonderland,
this Missoni-inspired ensuite features a
kaleidoscope of colour and pattern.

SO/ Auckland Hotel

AUCKLAND, NEW ZEALAND

Situated in the downtown Britomart district in the heart of the city, this luxurious urban avant-garde design blends the essence of the destination with the hotel's soul, bursting with local energy and magnificent views.

Freycinet Lodge

FREYCINET NATIONAL PARK, AUSTRALIA

Designed by local Hobart architects, Liminal Studio, this open-air ensuite is nestled in the surrounding native bushland and lined with curved Tasmanian timbers. Soaking in the bath and stargazing at the clear Tasmania night skies is an incredible way to finish a day in the national park and is perfectly paired with the hotel's turn-down service of handmade Tasmanian chocolates and beautiful Tasmanian single malt whisky.

THE
AMERICAS

Baccarat Hotel

NEW YORK CITY, NEW YORK, USA

The Baccarat Suite's spa-like white-marble bathroom features a deep, free-standing soaking tub, glass-walled shower and Italian robes. The Baccarat crystal MEMOIRE Elephant is priced at $99,500; there is only one available in the country for sale and it is at the Madison Avenue flagship store.

AKA Times Square

NEW YORK CITY, NY, USA
PENTHOUSE RESIDENCE

A quiet respite in the heart of one of the most the vibrant and thrilling areas of New York City, AKA Times Square's master bathroom in the 'crown jewel' Penthouse Residence is nearly the size of a standard NYC hotel room – providing the ultimate, spa-like experience at 18.58 square metres. Designed in 1893 by famed architect George Keister, the façade is designed in a Romanesque Revival manner, punctuated by Gothic and Renaissance details derived from German sources, marking the design's unique expression in a time of stylistic transition overall. The pampering doesn't stop there – the master bath features a sculptural, modern freestanding bathtub, oversized dual rain head shower behind a free-floating glass wall, and a double basin vanity featuring Bulgari amenities.

Civana Wellness Resort & Spa

CAREFREE, ARIZONA, USA

Nestled high in the Sonoran Desert and designed to exude calmness, this ensuite features a mid-century modern design incorporating a subtle colour scheme of natural tones and quality furnishings built from locally manufactured materials and millwork.

Four Seasons Hotel New York

Located at the city's most prestigious address, between Park Avenue and Madison Avenue, this ensuite features an elegant use of light, classical sense of form and modern mastery of method.

Mountain Shadows Resort

PARADISE VALLEY, ARIZONA, USA

Boasting iconic views of Camelback Mountains, this ensuite features exposed concrete ceilings, floor-to-ceiling glass, and modern Southwest design. A luxurious add-on to this experience is the Bath Butler who will deliver all the goodies for a luxe bubble bath, including a full-sized Herbivore Coconut Milk Bath Soak, bubble bath, chocolate-dipped strawberries, tealight candles, a full-sized candle and a bottle of wine.

The Knickerbocker Hotel

NEW YORK CITY, NEW YORK, USA
THE CARUSO SUITE

The Caruso Suite, fashioned to emulate the essence of its namesake, Enrico Caruso, the world-famous opera tenor, is home to one of the most lavish bathrooms in New York City. Featuring 13 slabs of marble, honed from Breccia Capraia, a rare and treasured Italian marble with dramatic violet veining, and weighing in at an astounding 4,000 pounds, the bathroom is dramatic and glamorous featuring veiled glass, and softly illuminated mirrors. Reminiscent of brush strokes in paintings by the masters, the bathroom marble's bold, lavish natural patterning assists in setting a dramatic atmosphere. Layered with exquisite detailing featuring a hint of rich purple throughout that echoes the colour story of the bathroom, accents of antique bronze tones and white gold leaf add a further elegant yet flamboyant language to this very elegant hidden gem.

Four Seasons Resort
The Biltmore Santa Barbara

SANTA BARBARA, CALIFORNIA

A favoured retreat of old Hollywood and America's elite
since it opened in 1927, this Spanish Colonial adobe
building with red roof tiles and graceful archways showcases
its historic ensuite featuring custom handcrafted furnishings,
art objects and treasures throughout.

The Vintages Trailer Resort

DAYTON, OREGON, USA

The Spartan Royal Mansion is a 10.9 meters long trailer, that dates back to 1956. Completely renovated to create a more traditional guestroom experience, it has a boho-chic style and boasts an ultra-cool private outdoor tub, perfect for stargazing while enjoying a relaxing soak, in addition to comfortable patio seating.

Tivoli Mofarrej São Paulo Hotel

SÃO PAULO, BRAZIL
PRESIDENTIAL SUITE

Located on the 22nd floor of the Tivoli Mofarrej São Paulo Hotel, The Mofarrej Presidential Suite is the epitome of sophistication and exclusivity. Boasting incredible city views with floor-to-ceiling windows, the largest suite in Latin America features a luxurious bath, spacious Jacuzzi, double rainfall showerheads and sauna.

Uxua Casa Hotel & Spa

BAHIA, BRAZIL

Designed using traditional techniques, reclaimed materials and antiques, all by local artisans, UXUA Casa Hotel & Spa's suites showcase a rustic open-air shower and vintage bathtub surrounded by fruit-bearing cacao trees in the garden.

Hotel Esencia

QUINTANA ROO, MEXICO
MASTER BEACH SUITES

Located directly on the ivory white sands of famous Xpu Ha beach, this ethereally white-washed bathroom features an in-room double bathtub "for two," perfectly positioned to enjoy stunning views of the Caribbean Sea, accompanied by an indoor and outdoor shower and a heated plunge pool.

The Spectator Hotel

Evoking the exuberance of the Jazz Age and the genteel glamour of the Old South, this sleek boutique hotel that is located in Charleston's bustling historic district features spa-like bathrooms outfitted with white marble and posh amenities. To truly enhance the luxury experience, ensuites are complete with over-sized double vanities, heated towel racks, floor-to-ceiling tiled showers and large tubs where baths can be drawn by a professionally trained personal butler.

The Cape, A Thompson Hotel

LOS CABOS, MEXICO

Featuring a rustic antique vibe with hints of a suave and modern feel, the open structure of the ensuite showcases a state-of-the-art 360-degree rain shower and freestanding copper-leafed tub which allows for perfect views of the crystal blue Sea of Cortez.

Castle Hot Springs

MORRISTOWN, ARIZONA, USA
THE SPRING BUNGALOWS

Designed for pure luxury and relaxation, this outdoor,
private, custom-made Sonoma stone tubs offers sweeping
views of the Bradshaw mountains and at night-time, skies
for stargazing. All bathtubs and showers across the resort
are filled with mineral-rich water pumped directly from
the resort's ancient, thermal hot springs.

Fairmont Pacific Rim Hotel

VANCOUVER, BC, CANADA
THE CHAIRMAN'S SUITE

The Chairman's Suite bathroom features a 152 square metre ensuite with a hand-carved deep jetted soaker tub, floor-to-ceiling windows and a private terrace, complete with a meditation pond, fire pit and private gazebo. It showcases fine Italian marble covering the floors, walls, and vanity. Other bathrooms on the property have spacious soakers, jetted tubs, and one has a tub that resembles an exotic ergonomic egg. While some of the tubs are cocooned in spa-like bathrooms, others have nothing but glass between them and the vast harbour and mountain views.

THE
CARIBBEAN

Amanera

PLAYA GRANDE,
DOMINICAN REPUBLIC

Situated on the rainforested Dominican Republic's north shore above the palm backed Playa Grande Beach, each spacious casita is crafted from the finest local materials, including teak wood, indigenous coral stone, Terrazzo flooring and striking contemporary furniture. Each room includes a bathroom with a freestanding bathtub, walk-in shower, skylights and a sliding door offering a beautiful view of the Caribbean jungle and the crystal water of the north Dominican Republic's Playa Grande beach.

The Ocean Club, A Four Seasons Resort, Bahamas

PARADISE ISLAND, BAHAMAS

Originally opened in 1962 as a hideaway for celebrities
and international elite traditional, the ensuites in this
low-rise Caribbean style building feature a masterful
mixing of rich woods and polished marble.

Club Med Punta Cana

PUNTA CANA, DOMINICAN REPUBLIC

Located on the island of Hispaniola and designed with wellness and comfort in mind, this spa-like ensuite features a rainfall shower, oversized bathtub, mood lighting and a private garden with plush daybeds.

Four Seasons Resort & Residences Anguilla

WEST END, ANGUILLA

Showcasing modern glamour with a tropical oasis backdrop, this beachfront ensuite showcases sophisticated and contemporary interiors with a relaxed chic sensibility and unique sense of place. Organic elements such as petrified-wood tables and travertine marble floors add a tasteful contrast to the geometric lines of the architecture.

W Costa Rica

GUANACASTE PROVINCE, COSTA RICA

Enveloped in a vast nature preserve teeming with
wildlife, overlooking the majestic Pacific Ocean and white
sand beaches, this sustainably designed and vibrant
ensuite draws in design elements of the surrounding
landscape and Costa Rica's surfing culture.

Rock House

PROVIDENCE, TURKS AND CAICOS

Blending elegantly into its rugged coastline and providing unsurpassed views and privacy in a handmade setting, this expansive ensuite incorporates limestone from the surrounding landscape for the epitome of sophistication and warmth, rich with Turks and Caicos history.

Zemi Beach House

SHOAL BAY VILLAGE, ANGUILLA
BEACHFRONT SUITE

Perched on Anguilla's Shoal Bay East, this ensuite boasts unparalleled views of the crystal blue waters, set in contemporary luxury blended with décor that is inspired by the island's rich tradition.

Spice Island
Beach Resort

SPICE ISLAND, GRENADA

Tucked along world-famous Grand Anse Beach, this enchanting marble ensuite features a stylish contemporary Caribbean design.

Round Hill Hotel & Villas

MONTEGO BAY, JAMAICA

Featuring a mix of traditional West Indian vernacular with a modern twist, this ensuite which merges indoors and outdoors, combines luxury fixtures with local materials, finished by local artisans, for an understated elegance.

UNITED
KINGDOM
&
EUROPE

Château De Le Treyne

LACAVE, FRANCE
LA FAVORITE

Overlooking the river Dordogne, Château de la Treyne's master suite, La Favorite, is situated in a 17th-century tower surrounded by 3 square kilometres of private parkland. Boasting views of the river and the French formal garden, the bathroom features underfloor heating and porcelain taps furnished by BERNARDAUD, a famous Limoges porcelain company.

COMO Castello Del Nero

TUSCANY, ITALY

At the heart of this historic 740-acre estate is a twelfth-century castle layered with Renaissance frescoes and contemporary design. With the rolling hills of Tuscany as a backdrop, this beautiful ensuite was originally the sitting room of the private apartment of Marchesa Anna Torregiani Frey, and features frescos by Giuseppe Giarrè dating from the late 1700s.

Château Pont Saint-Martin

LÉOGNAN, FRANCE

Located in the heart of the Crus Classés of Pessac-Léognan, this property is represented by a neo-Palladian castle, in evocative colours, with unique architecture in Bordeaux. The ensuite, which has been restored from the property's old cellar, consists of eclectic artifacts found in the region and markets around the world.

Château Lafaurie-Peyraguey

BOMMES, FRANCE

Structured by wooden alcoves and punctuated with a few colourful touches reminiscent of the polychromy of the wine, a sense of detail and harmony reigns over each ensuite with touches of Lalique crystal and vineyard views.

Gleneagles

AUCHTERARDER, SCOTLAND
THE ROYAL LOCHNAGAR SUITE

Offering uninterrupted views across the rolling Glendevon Hills and evoking the grandeur of a stately home, the Royal Suite boasts a traditional powder room, dressing room and a separate ensuite. The design team's inspiration for the space was led by a commitment to remain faithful to Gleneagles' origins and strong Scottish identity and to celebrate the property's rich and glamorous heritage.

Château Malromé

Located in the South of Gironde in the Entre-Deux-Mers region, Malromé is surrounded by fields, woods and vineyards in the town of Saint-André-du-Bois. The castle now offers a contemporary and heritage aesthetic framework thanks to the work of the architect Laurent Negretti and interior designer Isabelle Stanislas. The ensuite has walls covered with stretched silks with floral motifs, on which are lithographs by Henri de Toulouse-Lautrec which trace the intimate world of women working in the Closed Houses at the end of the 19th century.

Crillon le Brave

PROVENCE, FRANCE

Boasting inviting views of the stunning natural scenes of some of the most sought-after vineyards in France, each ensuite is unique with antique furniture and carefully selected artifacts. Featuring double vintage free-standing bathtubs with paw shaped feet and a champagne holder between them, this is the ultimate spot to relax and enjoy the ambiance from panoramic windows looking out to Mont Ventoux.

Hotel Punta Tragara

CAPRI, ITALY

Overlooking the landmark Faraglioni rock formations in the Tyrrhenian Sea, this ensuite was designed by legendary architect Le Courbusier to capture the timeless glamour of the island.

Royal Champagne Hotel & Spa

CHAMPILLON, FRANCE

Boasting an enviable location, situated right in the middle of the vineyards
that stripe the hills of Epernay and the historic villages of Champillon
and Hautvillers of Dom Pérignon fame, this modern ensuite draws design
inspiration from the heart of the surrounding area favouring natural materials
such as oak and stone to contrast with the interiors' graphic style. Pastel
shades blend with acid tones and classic notes, just as with a premier cru,
creating a sensory feeling of singular refinement.

Vora Hotel

SANTORINI, GREECE

Inspired by the local architecture with charming details such
as the recurring arches, the luxurious bathrooms feature blue
Gascoigne double sinks with Pierre Boon faucets and generous
showers. A mix of custom-made items by local craftspeople as
well as local materials such as black volcanic rocks and Vasaltis
marble, give the spaces its unique stamp.

Speicher 7

MANNHEIM, GERMANY

Once a spectacular granary built in
the 1950s, this ensuite has a modern
industrial design featuring a 12-metre
high silo, a bathtub and a shower.

San Luis Retreat Hotel & Lodges

AVELENGO, ITALY

An oasis of calm found hidden on the Avelengo plateau in South Tyrol and set around a natural private lake, this modern alpine-inspired ensuite has been designed using local wood, black slate, raw linen, handmade furniture, chrome taps and exposed natural wood beams.

Forestis

TYROL, AUSTRIA

Located on the southern slope of the Plose Mountain
at 1800 metres above sea level, this refuge for
relaxation is surrounded by dense mountain forests.
It was built using carbon neutral construction
methods that included the use of native materials
to reference the solitary location and contemplative
connection with nature.

Amanruya

BODRUM, TURKEY

Set in an enchanting setting above the Aegean coast with the tranquil ambience of an Ottoman village, each standalone pavilion features a spacious Hammam inspired bathroom. Carved out of white marble with natural lighting, oversized 'his and hers' vanities, rain shower and a free-standing designer bath, the ensuite boasts views of the surrounding ancient olive groves and Mediterranean pine forest.

Domaine des Etangs

MASSIGNAC, FRANCE

Experience the grandeur of the 11th century chateau and take in the surrounding views of the expansive grounds from the enormous roll-top bath. The beautiful bathroom, intricately designed and perfected by Isabelle Stanislas, designer to the French President, is bright and spacious with windows opening to the expansive property grounds of woodland, lakes and dotted with art installations.

L'Arlatan

ARLES, FRANCE

Recognised as being Arles' most lavish hotel since
as early as the Middle Ages, each ensuite offers an
explosion of colour, light and contemporary design
with unrivaled charm, featuring unique works of art with
almost two million fragments of handmade mosaic tiles.

Elounda Peninsula
All Suite Hotel

ELOUNDA, GREECE

Decorated with luxurious finishes
including a marble bath, a sauna, and
a massage room, this bathroom boasts
beautiful views across the iridescent
Aegean Sea and Sitia mountains.

Ajwa Hotel Sultanahmet

ISTANBUL, TURKEY

Set within the fabled Old City of Istanbul, a
UNESCO World Heritage Site, this marble ensuite
features hand-painted tiles that are inspired by
their unique counterparts in Istanbul and provide a
vivid insight into the city beyond the hotel walls.

Grand Central Hotel

BELFAST, UK

Located at the heart of the enchanting city of Belfast, this ensuite combines contemporary design and grandeur with local Belfast authenticity and features a Bespoke Soak bath experience and bath menu with a world-class bath butler service to create the perfect backdrop for an indulgent soak.

Calilo

Made from local marble and
shaped and sculpted by local
craftsmen, the bathrooms in Calilo's
suites are truly extraordinary. The
result is a kaleidoscopic bathroom,
with a deep bathtub carved from a
single piece of marble.

Hotel Barrière

CHAMPS-ELYSÉES, FRANCE
ARC DE TRIOMPHE

Located on the Champs-Elysées, the ultra-luxurious Arc de Triomphe signature suite features unmatched views of Paris' most iconic avenue and the Arc de Triomphe from every vantage point in the expansive suite—including the bathtub! With elegant grey marble and silver fixtures, this is one of the most Instagram-worthy bathrooms in Paris.

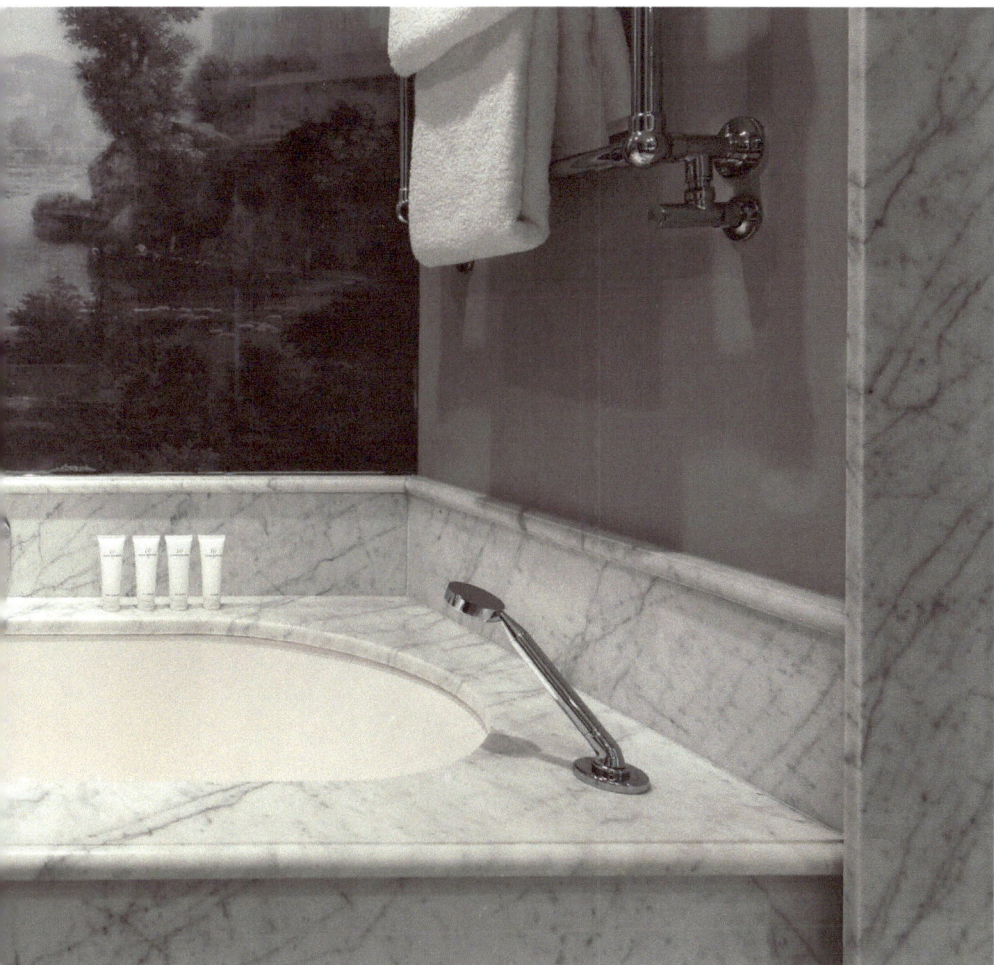

L'Apogée Courchevel

Designed as a mini-chalet for warmth, relaxation and incomparable luxury amongst its extraordinary Alpine landscape, this ensuite showcases separate "his and hers" sink units, a deep-soaking bathtub with gold taps carved from the finest marble, and is complete with a private in-room sauna, steam room, jacuzzi, and glamorous floor to ceiling gold mosaic adorning the walls.

Hotel De Crillon

PARIS, FRANCE

Offering breathtaking views over Paris and its landmarks including the Eiffel Tower, Grand Palais, Musée d'Orsay and Place de la Concorde, this ensuite was designed by Karl Lagerfeld with his unique vision of French-chic and modernity. A two-ton bathtub carved from a single block of Carrera marble serves as the extravagant centrepiece of this 'fashion' bathroom.

Hotel Metropole

MONTE-CARLO, MONACO
PRESTIGE SUITE

Renowned for its luxury and charm, Hotel Metropole's Prestige Suite features a luxurious marble and gold bathroom with massive shower and mosaic flooring connected to a spacious walk-in closet. An ultra-lavish amenity, the Prestige Suite bathroom includes complimentary, full-size Hermès perfumes/colognes and bath products along with SkinJay essential oils for showering amidst natural customised fragrances.

Argentario Golf Resort & Spa

TUSCANY, ITALY
LOCKER COTTAGE

Featuring a Turkish bath and a separate shower, the interiors of Locker Cottage have been designed by Milan-based Andrea Fogli to create the feel of a Tuscan country house with a glamorous and eclectic touch.

Rosewood London Hotel

LONDON, ENGLAND, UK
MANOR HOUSE

A stunning circular soaking tub hewn from a single piece of Carrera marble takes centre stage in the suite's expansive master bathroom, which also provides a walk-in rain shower, waterfall feature, marble bench and his-and-her vanities.

Summer Lodge
Country House Hotel

DORSET, ENGLAND
IVY COTTAGE

Set in a charming stone-built Dorset chalet, this ensuite encapsulates the finest in intimate English countryside design with an abundant Austen-esque romance.

The Scarlet Hotel

MAWGAN PORTH, UNITED KINGDOM
INDULGENT ROOM

The Indulgent Rooms at the Scarlet Hotel offer an
open plan bathroom with a free standing bath, a
large monsoon shower and a separate toilet.

University Arms Hotel

Situated in a landmark hotel located in the historic heart of Cambridge, this gorgeous bathroom lies within the original domed turrets, featuring large windows, roll-top claw-foot baths, dark tiled flooring, and Cambridge blue accents throughout with views overlooking Parker's Piece.

Tivoli Carvoeiro
Algarve Resort

LAGOA, PORTUGAL

This lavish open bathroom offers views
overlooking the Atlantic Ocean on the
Vale Covo cliffside.

Terre Blanche Hôtel

TOURRETTES, FRANCE
TERRE BLANCHE PRESTIGE VILLA

The master bedroom of the Prestige Villa has a superb marble bathroom that is equipped with heated marble floors, an above-ground bath, a shower, a double water closet, and double sinks. The bathroom opens onto a terrace fitted with a jacuzzi with a magnificent view over the hills of the Pays de Fayence.

Villa Lopez

MYKONOS, GREECE

Boasting dramatic seascape views, this impressive ensuite features a marble shower, twin vanity and an expansive bathtub looking across the Aegean Sea.

AFRICA

Borana Lodge

LAIKIPIA, KENYA
LENGISHU HOME

Lengishu is the latest exclusive-use home to open on the Borana Lodge in Northern Kenya, the country's newest and most successful rhino sanctuary. This stunning retreat has a gorgeous bathtub overlooking spectacular views across the Laikipia plains. Blending seamlessly into its surroundings, this is the perfect spot to relax, to watch the sunset and to spot incredible wildlife.

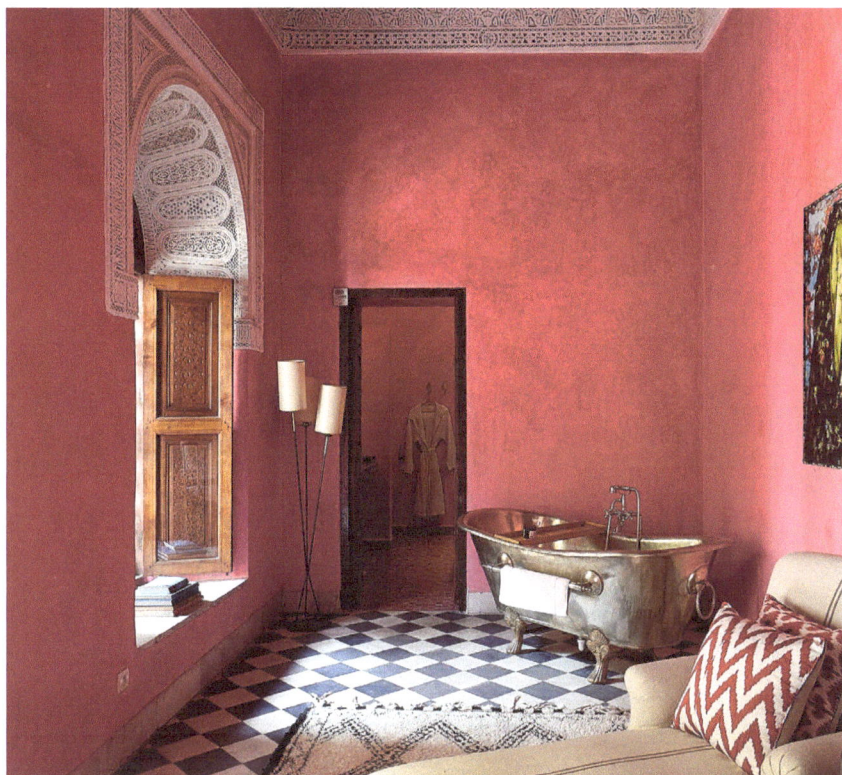

El Fenn

MARRAKECH, MOROCCO

This stunning deep marble bath is surrounded by exotic green Tadelakt walls with polished lime plastering, using pure natural pigments from the medina. A riot of colour, the décor is Moroccan with both contemporary and retro twists which showcase works from Vanessa Branson's private art collection and a huge Venetian mirror. With a separate additional shower room and water closet, creature comforts include dual sinks and a monsoon power shower.

Four Seasons Resort Seychelles

MAHE ISLAND, SEYCHELLES

Perched on a granite hillside in a tree-house villa that overlooks the turquoise waters of Petite Anse Bay, a large infinity plunge pool wraps around a glass-wall and features a deep-soaking bath and large rain shower.

La Mamounia

MARRAKECH, MOROCCO

The history of La Mamounia is permeated with
art in its various forms and their marble ensuites
boast ornate Moorish-inspired tile work, deep
soaking tubs and natural, luxurious toiletries.

La Sultana

Located in the heart of the historical
Medina, this oasis of calm showcases
authentic Moroccan craftsmanship.

Makumu Private Game Lodge

KLASERIE PRIVATE NATURE RESERVE
SOUTH AFRICA

Makumu, which translates to 'endless view' in the Xitsonga language, boasts floor to ceiling windows with unparalleled views of the African bush and the opportunity to spot wildlife from the comfort of your bath. The ensuite features beautiful patterns, designs and tiling influenced by the Bushman, Ndebele and Zulu tribes of Africa, and is lit entirely by candlelight at night, creating a romantic atmosphere that is one with nature.

Le Grand Jardin

Set against the vineyard backdrop of heritage-rich Stellenbosch, this green marble tub which was imported from India's Brahma Granitech, is inspired by the villa's surrounding which boast 500 rose bushes, lavender fields and the tranquility of rolling lawns.

Morkuru Beach Lodge

DE HOOP NATURE RESERVE, SOUTH AFRICA

Situated along the unspoilt coastline of the De Hoop Nature
Reserve, this luxurious ensuite was inspired by the surrounding
towering white sand dunes lapped by the Indian Ocean,
limestone cliffs, rock pools and coastal fynbos.

Matetsi Victoria Falls

MATETSI PRIVATE GAME
RESERVE, ZIMBABWE

Acclaimed for its exquisite
contemporary build featuring local
beaten-copper, carved wood, polished
earth finishes and hand-made
contemporary African furnishings, this
ensuite offers plenty of space to indulge
in the wild with sliding doors framing
views of the mighty Zambezi river.

Okuti Resort

MOREMI GAME RESERVE, BOTSWANA

Built amidst the wilderness of one of Botswana's
prime game viewing regions, this ensuite has an
indoor and outdoor that is exceptionally unique
in style and architecture reflecting the Maunachira
River which flows in front of the camp.

Singita Boulders Lodge

SABI SANDS GAME RESERVE, SOUTH AFRICA

Inspired by the geometry of the boulders on which it rests, the bathrooms at Boulders Lodge are an inviting oasis where organic interiors integrate seamlessly with the raw African beauty outside. The surrounding landscape and animals can be seen and enjoyed from every angle of the bathroom including from the serenity of the stunning stone bathtubs, making for a truly immersive safari experience.

Sabi Sabi Bush Lodge

SOUTH AFRICA

Looking out onto the unspoiled bushveld and
exuding luxury and comfort in the contemporary
Bush Lodge style, this ensuite features rich textures
within its myriad of details, including raw grass
wallpaper, smooth floor finishes and leadwood
sculptures mirroring the natural environment.

Six Senses Zil Pasyon

FÉLICITÉ ISLAND, SEYCHELLES
HIDEAWAY POOL VILLAS

Set amongst the towering rocks and
boulders of Félicité Island, this spacious
ensuite was designed to echo the island's
epic natural form, featuring a swing in front
of a bathtub with glorious ocean views, a
separate rain shower and contemporary
architecture and interiors that perfectly
complement the landscape of the island.

Makanyi Private Game Lodge

TIMBAVATI RESERVE, SOUTH AFRICA

Protected by an imposing grove of marula trees, this prime safari lodge features a stylish decor that connects to the land with heavy slub linen, taxidermy with rural finds and brass fittings with modern chrome.

Somalisa Camp

HWANGE NATIONAL PARK, ZIMBABWE

Featuring a traditional Victorian style water closet, twin copper sinks which sit on a rustic piece of local Acacia wood, and a 2.6 metre copper wrapped rolltop bath, the elegant authentic contemporary African style is infused by natural wood, locally mined copper, and organic features of the surrounding wilderness. Perfectly situated to provide 270 degree views of the bush and elephant waterhole whilst bathing, this open plan offers incredible bushland views with the utmost privacy.

Saseka Tented Camp

SOUTH AFRICA

Influenced by the romantic narrative of tented camps from yesteryear, the elevated ensuite has been reimagined with a gentle nod to nostalgia to offer a truly immersive safari experience.

The St. Regis Mauritius Resort

LE MORNE, MAURITIUS

With its spacious ocean-facing terrace, private tempered plunge pool and direct access to a 143 metre beachfront, this ensuite's spacious volume is further enhanced by marble surfaces, a bathtub with spray jets, a separate shower and an inside-outside design concept in which the facades slide away to reveal ocean views stretching as far as the eye can see.

Sasaab

SAMBURU, KENYA

Majestically situated on the high banks of the
Ewaso Nyiro River, this plush permanent tent
offers an open-air bathroom with commanding
views across the arid landscape of the Northern
Frontier District from its private plunge bath.

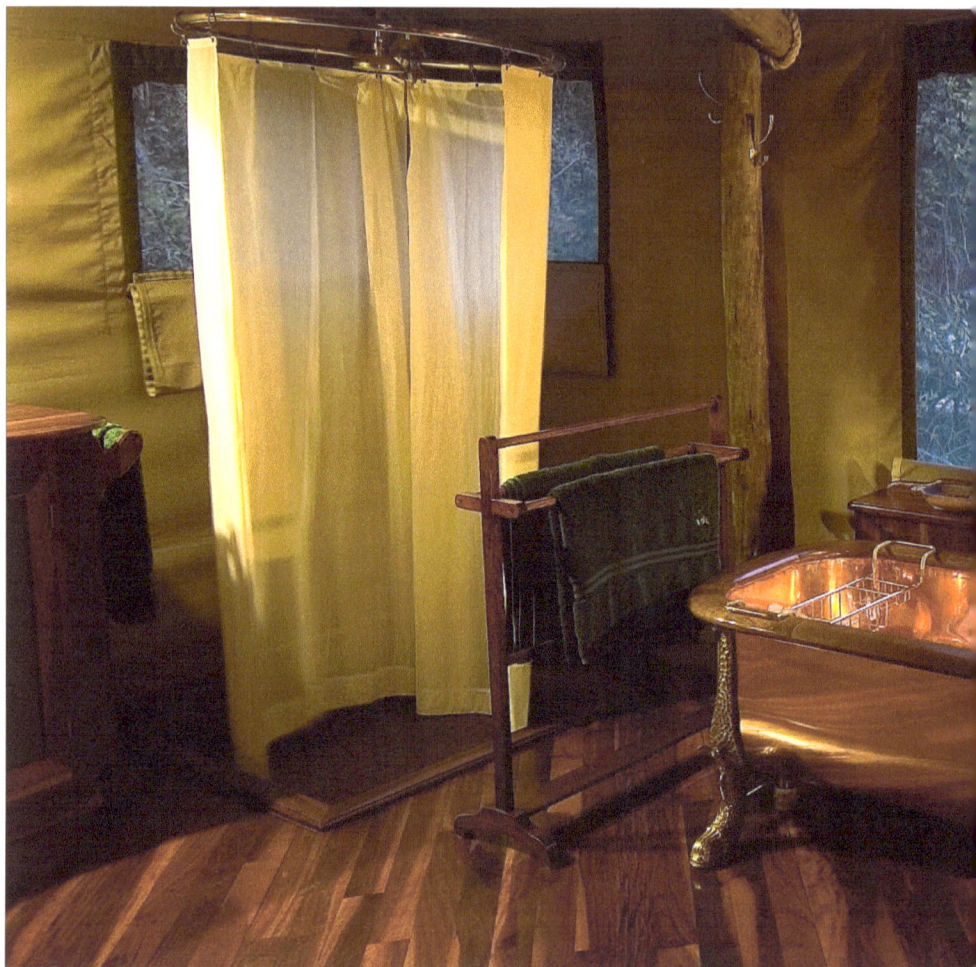

Wilderness Safaris' Abu Camp

OKAVANGO DELTA, BOTSWANA

Looking out over a large lagoon, an imaginative use of canvas has created a unique and luxurious style of bathing featuring a copper bath and a plunge pool sunk into the elevated teak deck where elephants can be seen at a watering hole just meters away.

The Oyster Box Hotel

DURBAN, SOUTH AFRICA
PRESIDENTIAL SUITE

Split over two levels with a private
lift, the Presidential Suite boasts two
separate his and hers lavish marble
bathrooms with unsurpassed sea views
for the ultimate luxury and tranquility.

The Twelve Apostles Hotel & Spa

CAPE TOWN, SOUTH AFRICA
GRAND MASTER SUITE

Encompassing a free-standing antique marble bath, cool white marble floors with underfloor heating, this ensuite showcases antique mirrors, mosaics and finely carved panels that adorn the floors, walls and ceiling.

Wilderness Safaris' Mombo Camp

OKAVANGO DELTA, BOTSWANA

Featuring indoor and outdoor showers and a copper tub with brass fittings, this ensuite offers one of the best opportunities for wildlife viewing, whether enjoying a bath or brushing teeth, inquisitive animals are likely to be spotted at any moment.

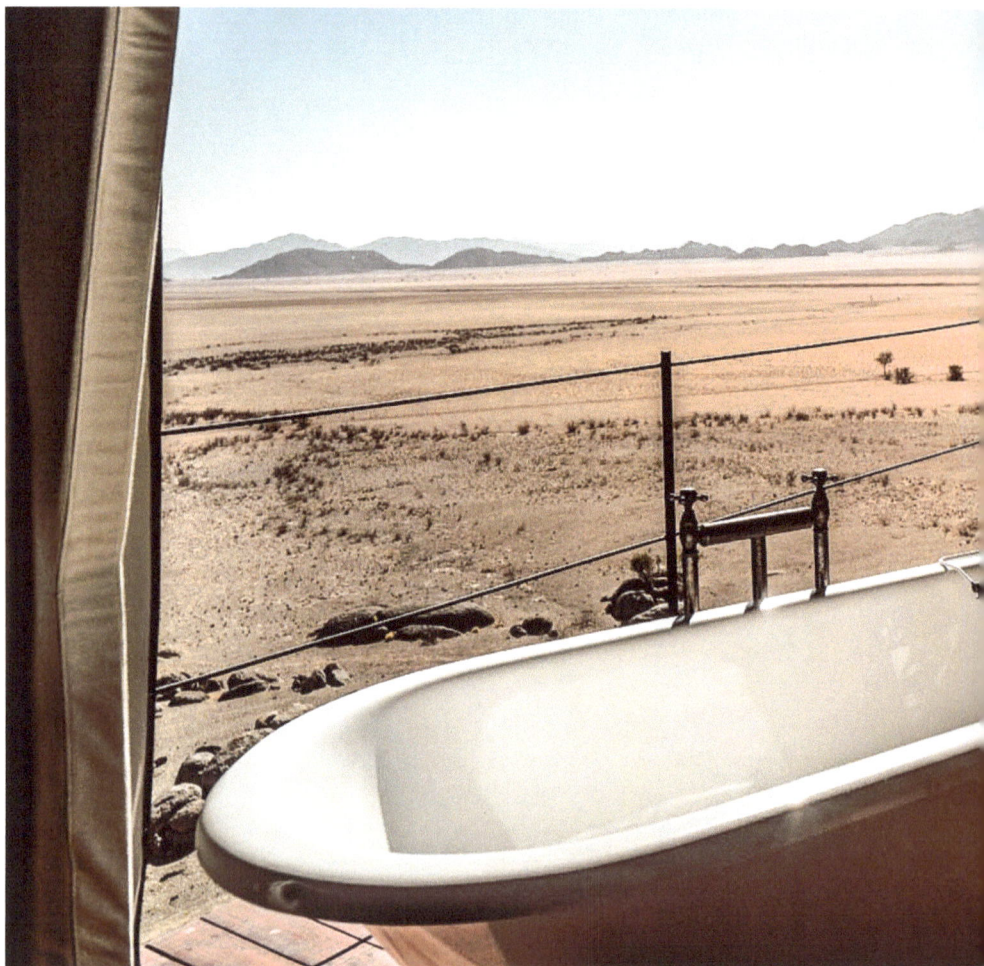

Zannier Hotels Sonop

KARAS REGION, NAMIBIA

Built entirely on stilts connected through sturdy elevated wooden decks atop a group of boulders, affording awe-inspiring 360 degree views of the Southern Namib Desert, each luxury tent boasts floor to ceiling windows which offer magnificent views of the desert while soaking in a large, luxurious bathtub. A rain shower, double vanity and beautiful dressing table complete the space with thoughtful touches such as tiny flasks and unique combs, whilst the materials and colour palette have been selected to complement the desert terrain and blend into the boulders.

MIDDLE
EAST

Four Seasons Hotel Kuwait at Burj Alshaya

KUWAIT

Situated in the heart of Kuwait City featuring a modern glass exterior with mashrabiya lattice work in a traditional Arabic pattern dating to the Middle Ages, this ensuite showcases cutting-edge interiors with a warm colour palette and carefully chosen textures and touches of Kuwaiti style and ambiance.

Anantara The Palm Dubai Resort

DUBAI, UAE
OVER WATER VILLAS

Blending Asian inspiration with idyllic views of the Arabian Gulf, this ensuite features a large sized bathtub and a soothing rain shower system. Set amidst a glass viewing panel, this ensuite reveals exotic underwater glimpses.

The Norman Tel Aviv

ISRAEL

Situated in the heart of Tel Aviv, this sanctuary of calm in the heart of the beating metropolis brings unprecedented sophistication and boutique character that capture the timeless elegance of the 1920s, featuring antique-inspired charm and glamour with contemporary art and technologies.

Alila Jabal Akhdar

OMAN

Perched over 2000 metres above sea level, the Alila Jabal Akhdar luxurious ensuites provide access overlooking a dramatic gorge and with views of the Al Hajar mountains. With an iconic design inspired by ancient forts, traditional Omani construction techniques using local stones are combined with contemporary architecture. Within the stone exteriors, the resort's unique expression of minimalist style is infused with warmth and colours that reflect the region's ethnic influence. Authentic elements of Omani design decorate the interiors, such as copper ornaments, and handmade pottery from Bahla, for which the town is famed.

Palazzo Versace

DUBAI, UAE

True to the roots of the renowned Italian fashion house, the hotel's interiors reimagine the Versace lifestyle through the contemporary eyes of Donatella Versace, its Artistic Director. With 215 Italianate bedrooms and 169 luxury residences, accommodation immerses guests into the brand's renowned glamour with furniture and fabrics designed and tailor-made by the House of Versace exclusively for the hotel. Versace icons abound throughout, with motifs such as the famed Medusa, classical friezes and the House's legendary prints present at every turn. Bathrooms feature handcrafted mosaics and Carrara marble tiling – the ultimate backdrop to the walk-in rainforest showers.

Four Seasons Hotel Abu Dhabi at Al Maryah Island

ABU DHABI, UAE

This 34-storey glass tower blends urban chic and understated luxury into its light-filled ensuite, which features an art-inspired design aesthetic with locally sourced elements and artwork that pays homage to the spirit of the United Arab Emirates.

INDEX

COUNTRY INDEX

COUNTRY INDEX (CONT.)

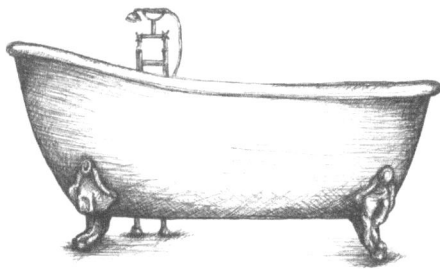

ACKNOWLEDGEMENTS

Retreat Magazine
presents

Bath Envy

THE WORLD'S MOST ICONIC HOTEL BATHS

Editor
Molly Martin

Published by
Retreat Magazine

Design & Illustration
Kimberly Randall

ISBN : 978-0-6488292-4-9

For more, please visit www.retreatmag.com.

www.ingramcontent.com/pod-product-compliance
Lightning Source LLC
Chambersburg PA
CBHW041957090426
42811CB00014B/1522